INVISIBLE TENDER

INVISIBLE TENDER

JENNIFER CLARVOE

With an introduction by J. D. McClatchy

FORDHAM UNIVERSITY PRESS
New York

Copyright © 2000 by Fordham University Press

All rights reserved. No part of this publication may be reproduced, stored in a retrieval system, or transmitted in any form or by any means—electronic, mechanical, photocopy, recording, or any other—except for brief quotations in printed reviews, without the prior permission of the publisher.

Library of Congress Cataloging-in-Publication Data

Clarvoe, Jennifer.
    Invisible tender / Jennifer Clarvoe ; with an introduction by J. D. McClatchy.—1st ed.
      p. cm.
    ISBN 0-8232-2089-3 (hardcover)—ISBN 0-8232-2090-7 (pbk.)
    I. Title.
PS3553.L3444 I58   2000
811'.6—dc21   00-042949

Printed in the United States of America
01 02 03 04 5 4 3 2
First Edition

This book is dedicated to the memory of my grandparents,
Alfred Shohl and Florence Cozad Shohl,
Kenneth Scott and Aurelia Grether Scott,
and to my son, Sam.

CONTENTS

Acknowledgments ix
Introduction xi
I. First Shapes 1
    2217 *Platenstrasse* 3
    Celery: Victorian Cross-Section 5
    Family 6
    Parts of a Bomb Poem 7
    Deck 7 9
    Ship's Lounge 10
    Vanity 12
    Gaze 14
    Answers 15
    Up Fish Ranch Road 17
    Lining 18
    The Lower Cottage 20
    Cracks 22
    Tracks 24
    Conscience Rocks 25
    Francesca & Paolo 29
    Picnic 31

II. Songs of Multiplication and Division 33
    Thou Art Translated 35
    Distant Heart 40
    Flight 41
    Adam's Hand 42
    Song of Multiplication and Division 43
    Private, Offhand Sestina 45
    The Anguish 47
    Leave-Taking 48

Thread of Song   49
Mock Sestina   50
Echolocation: The Whale   52
Lesson   54
Mine   55
Ohio: Unused Fireplace   60
A Company   62
Birdnotes   65
Landscape Lit by an Apricot   67
Ruth's Garden   69
Household Prayer   71

ACKNOWLEDGMENTS

Grateful acknowledgment to the editors of the magazines in which versions of the poems in this volume first appeared: "2217 Platenstrasse" in *The Partisan Review;* "Vanity" in *The Agni Review;* "Up Fish Ranch Road" in *Pavement;* "Answers," "Lining," and "The Lower Cottage" in *Berkeley Poetry Review;* "Thou Art Translated" in *Pequod;* "Adam's Hand" in *Verse;* "Song of Multiplication and Division," "A Company," and "Birdnotes" in *Poetry Northwest;* "Mine" in *The Ohio Review;* "Mock Sestina" in *Boston Phoenix;* "Ruth's Garden" in *The Yale Review.*

Thanks to my parents for their support, and to my friends for their advice and encouragement. For their immeasurable contributions, my thanks to Robert Pinsky and James McMichael.

INTRODUCTION
J. D. McClatchy

As it is light that makes color, it is perspective makes a poem. Not *poetry*, the pageant where soul is carried on the shoulders of language. But a successful poem, one that both pleases and puzzles, depends on angles, on the geometries of observation. Metaphor—seeing one thing as another—is perspective. So is form. Crisp stanzas or a runny wedge of free verse give the material they are forwarding not only the dynamics of a poetic voice but the long vistas and moral bearings of divergent traditions. Even at the most basic level of structure and tone, the way a poet enters and leaves her subject and the way she addresses it—these too are matters of perspective. And how we are in turn expected to regard the poet is also of her making. In fact, from the root of *perspective* branch other terms—*spy* or *skeptic*, the ability either to divine or despise, *horoscope* or *speculation*—that may help define a poet's stated or unconscious intentions. "Art is limitation," said Chesterton. "The essence of every picture is the frame."

Jennifer Clarvoe crops her pictures severely, then frames them in shadowboxes. Her poems are taut, skittish, equivocal. They offer themselves with a marked reluctance, eager to turn back in on their own mysteries. They are, in other words, *limited*, if by that figure of speech we signal their fascination with the boundaries between now and never, with a controlled but unpredictable seeing. In her bottomless poem "Thou Art Translated," Clarvoe even cites the Renaissance architectural theorist Sebastiano Serlio, a favorite of Francis I at Fontainebleau and the author of treatises on architecture and perspective that became pattern-books for Europe. His work was translated into English in 1611, and it is to this fact the poet alludes in a passage bristling with inferential detail and self-revelation:

*You must work round about
from step to step, always following
this rule, by the which you cannot fail,*

says Serlio, on shadows, "Translated
out of Italian into Dutch and out of Dutch
into Englifh. Entreating of Perfpective

which is, Infpection, or looking into,
by fhortening of the fight." I have shewed
many kinds of goings up,

but there are other kinds. I would like to rely
on the grand geometric assurances
one could voice in 1611—a line

a plan, its implementation. Things from another time
or in translation welcome
an understanding of something

that is not there,
that insinuates, proliferates like honeysuckle
painted over wood.

"The border," she says later, "is Doubt or Gravity or Sleep." And her effort throughout is to *shorten the sight*, to shear off the golden fleece of habit, of customary seeing. Her poems dart. I am reminded that the Arabic word for *thirst* can also mean *voice, echo, corpse, brain,* or *owl,* and that the word for *dictionary* also means *ocean.* Clarvoe's dictionary is awash with ways to make the things we think we know into other things we've not yet fancied but come to crave. Her poems do what isn't expected of them. They are continually leaping into dream states, or ascending to the sublime, or undoing their own grand assurances. In other words, they are a mirror of desire.

As you turn the pages of *Invisible Tender*—a perfect term for transactions of the spirit with the world this book records—you couldn't predict the next poem's setting. Each time, it's like waking up in a strange room, or a familiar one our dreams have momentarily obscured. It might be a soap opera set, a sonogram, a bird feeder, an ocean liner, or the corner of Putnam and Green. Just as unlikely are the directions in which Clarvoe may turn her narratives. The petrified forest with which one poem begins yields finally to a "marriage on the rocks" and love's broken crystal. If there is a domestic tug in her poems—the suburban home and child are recurrent props—there is no unearned sentiment. Everywhere her anarchic wit and mordant irony undarn the socks. Let me offer one large example: her long poem "Mine" is the most astonishing poem about childbirth I've read. One winces and clenches just reading it, and yet it is as eerie and exhilarating a tour of the premises as can be imagined.

If I have stressed her estrangements, I don't want to underestimate her charm. Her poem "Birdnotes" is the stuff of a short story by Chekhov or Munro. It starts with a small event already comically exaggerated:

> In the village, a single bird can be an event,
> can be news—just as the appearance
> of an available heterosexual male
> between the ages of 22 and 60
> can be news. It is news here, for example,
> when a Baltimore oriole shows up at the feeder,
> or a scarlet tanager (a pair of them!).

The sightings grow more exotic, the comedy more slapstick: "the poor lost emu on a rampage / through the village—definitely news, / moreso when finally lassoed by the chair / of the Philosophy Department." Then suddenly, everything turns tender, "news to write to sweethearts." The constricted life yet yields its wonders. There's a report of herons. Had she heard? Yes, there are the nests, the nestlings, the open beaks. The crowd swells, the traffic congests. It's a scene from Jane Austen:

> It's news, it's news.
> Now, here, with the riverside traffic blocked so folks
> on bicycles and rollerblades glide by—
> a brightly-colored, mushroom-helmeted species,
> many with the characteristic black
> fingerless gloves and shiny kneepads, gliding
> by in packs, in ones, twos—this one, now,
> skates past my bench in purple sleeveless T,
> sky-blue shorts, white baseball cap. She carries
> a cup of coffee from Au Bon Pain. There, perched
> easily on the brim, her orange parrot
> looks on the world with a somewhat jaded eye,
> for this is a city—and this is not news,
> this is nothing, isn't it? Nothing I
> or anyone would write home from the city
> to my sweetheart, in the village, if I had one.

The birders become birds, the observers a sight. All's reversed—or, as this poet would say, translated—and the little nothing becomes the all there is. In the line of poets from Frost to Bishop, from May Swenson to Kay Ryan, Jennifer Clarvoe is drawn to the idiosyncratic. To see is to seize, to take "broken, rotting, shambling things" and make a planetary system of them, to slip the pearl from its string and strip it to the bit of grit it started as. She is a moralist of the ups-and-downs, the ins-and-outs.

Like Bishop too, who was a canny allegorist, Clarvoe knows how to extend and deepen the ordinary. "Tracks" is an extravagance, a dream skating-party of instincts that draws blood. And in her wise "Cracks," for instance, an old cottage—the lock broken, and wind rattling the panes—serves her as a brain:

> Anything can get in—
> the wind, a bad idea—
>
> a *good* idea—but what
> is there to feed it here?

What indeed! While a nuthatch kibitzes, a titmouse "knocks and knocks— / one seed against the frame." Like Wallace Stevens's scholar of a single idea, this small bird is Clarvoe's appropriate—the word is contained in the bird's name—muse. Or "Lining," perhaps my favorite poem in this collection, an exquisite fable of the mind: how we read and what we read for. It ends with its eye on the very page we are reading from, and the poet's sharp, glinting words:

> There is a question
>
> of pain. Or permeability
> to question. Sometimes
> the mind rains through,
> its percussive this-es,
> all its silver skewers
> pins in a map
>
> minutely displacing the map;
> so not this, paper
> obscure through the glitter.
> She isn't here, but around
> here, in a deep rain
> disappearing.

These lovely, elusive lines brood on multiplications and divisions. The silver lining of Jennifer Clarvoe's imagination, for all its minute displacements and disappearing acts, promises to shine brilliantly in our poetry—not around here, but *here* and now.

I

First Shapes

2217 Platenstrasse

I go back by counting lampposts out of the fog—
seven is the length of the street by morning,
bottle-green posts against the gray. Shining,

the posts will spill the light before the street,
the street before the vegetable man's cart
delivers his bright fruit. *Blutorangen*,

oranges bruised garnet; and *Zuckermelone*,
we learn to click and pucker over the dark
small watermelons. Yes, we buy the vegetables,

but the names, the colors, are gifts. He saves *Blumenkohl*
for Timothy who is teething. Cauliflower,
flower cabbage, *Blumenkohl*. Given—

but how do we hold them? We kids just won't eat
brussels sprouts we bought as *Rosenkohl*.
Before dinner, we can't help it, we argue names,

any names, *Bully, Cry-baby*, racketing out
into the street, where we sing over each other
Don't run over me! Don't run over me—

in true kid's cadence, hot, indefatigable
see-sawing scorn—so that the random traffic
screeched with us. And how we needed that screech,

the song about our danger—so we could chase
danger, as if each car hauled in a future
we didn't want, some name, the engine feeding

us to plugs, cranks, shocks—chase it through the frame
in the old home movie that catches in the projector,
flares and caramelizes, burnt out to the edges

—so we could chase it away. Oblivious, wobbly
from laughing, we dance down slower revolutions,
like the scissor-grinder, who rides his bike

in one place, sharpening, humming. Silver street,
flat street, it must have been one or the other, or both
at different times. Silver like rain on the street,

flat like rain. On rainy nights flower vendors
come up in the stairwells with sugary freesia, mimosa.
Bouquets that glisten like names that have unloosened

their sense of obligation, those never tokens
by which you sense how much just is not given,
or not given again. And these remain

in flux, dissolving into wishes, wishes
crystallizing into gifts. Like this
silver like rain on the street, flat like rain.

Celery: Victorian Cross-Section

Light slips down its surface like the slicing's
memory, disconnecting into the sink in rings—
rings echoed by the outer fluted ridges
like thick petals, like ruffles threaded through
stiff silk, green silk with a cream white lining
meticulously pinked and perforated,
crimped to quintessence of pucker and snip, tuck, quill—

here an almost reptilian precision
hints at potential batwing, incisor, claw
suggests a nest of incubating dragons,
skeletons compressed, minutely curling
tail around tail, devolving to the core's
dense vegetable yellow. Oh what a snap-
shot's split-second, lid lifted, and these hints
breathing into the air a metallic tang.

FAMILY

One probably hears about it.
One, wire, recognizes.
One holds her bones up next to each other.
One insists, grinding the clutch.
One would powder and powder.
One would ask out of the back of the throat.
One refuses.
One is so sad.

One is helpful all of a sudden.
One turns.
One shimmers; hiccups.
One puts on a tie and keeps finding a place for his hands.
One breathes the old purple.
One nods because no one speaks loud enough anymore.
One doesn't approve, but trusts.
One is so sure.

Parts of a Bomb Poem

We thought our part, the kids' part, was to play
on the grass across the street from school, as if
late morning sun would always find us out
away from desks, as if this were our real
recess. To play as if we didn't know

we were waiting, like the grown-ups on the base,
for the scare to clear. But then the gangs
brought it home. Interminable inspection
at the gates, the long lines of cars, the families
re-collecting. Each day we almost thought

a guard would straighten up from behind the last
seat on the bus, balancing out in front
some lunchbox. That's what a bomb was.
Something you couldn't find in something you knew.
The abandoned car we never saw abandoned

maybe grew there, appeared like some flower that blooms
one night a year, approached in that terrific
silence by photographers. The date
our base was targeted, people went on vacation
all at once and far enough away

to make it seem an excuse for an expedition—
like our trips to Bonn, or to see the Strasbourg clock,
or to Hameln, where they hold the Pied Piper pageant
each Sunday in the square. We wanted to be
the kids running into the mountain, the funny doomed

rats in gray hoods. A bomb really did blow up
in the men's room at the old Farben building.
When my father worked there, the year before,
we never saw more than the door where we picked him up.
I can't even locate the year, or years

when it must have hit me that other kids
knew more about their fathers than his going
to work in the morning before we had to get up;
coming home tired with an empty thermos;
and after we were in bed, moving through rooms

turning lights off. In the dark, we heard
the piano making a music he never wrote down.
Some nights there was no music. Lights going out.
Countries we weren't allowed to visit. Bombs.
An office without windows in Defense.

Three quarter notes, a whole note, quarter rest?
The piano light goes on. *I see the moon,
and the moon sees me*, we used to play and sing
a long time ago, before the time overseas,
together at the piano, his arms around mine,

his left hand lower, right higher on the keys;
I just played on the white notes with one thumb.
The old basement piano in the first
home. But the gradual, inevitable explosions;
the little mimic flashcubes joke, joke.

Circle it in the pictures. What fuse, what match?
Home for vacation, vacation away from home.
A marriage, this climb, that job, the explanation—
parts loosening into the air, sparks, cinders, clouds—
and the first, unnoticed shape forever lost.

Deck 7

This is leisurely, leisurely on sea-legs
until the corner's grabbed rail, when with laughed jags
on the oblique tactic, we and the wind waltz

to the next turn where the wall tilts
up to us and we slap sideways, exposed,
slow to the middle distance, the hard haul pushed

past to the last seize, thrown
together with the wind alone
behind us, tumbling. We tumble. Our legs work
backwards as we almost
fall, tread water in advance
of the idea of water over the rail,
                                    and the last
clutch, instinct, not sight, we touch
home, the walk's start,
and leisurely, leisurely, each heart
lets the running feet run down, coincide
with the even, protected stride, against the ship's side.

Ship's Lounge

The ginger-ale glass' elegantly sliding
across the table seems to carry along
Grandma's voice, to underline "their shoes
worn out with dancing." How it clicks the rim
not too hard. The liquid never leaves
the horizontal. Waits a beat for the glass
to regain poise and then unlevels back
a polished path. "And in every boat there rowed
a handsome prince, all of whom were waiting"
—as if it will never spill—"for the twelve."
Jon and I lean closer to the glass,
chins to the table, but we wouldn't dream
of interrupting. Time and the ocean. Time
rocks and rocks the seemingly rimless days
and Grandma reads. She keeps an eye on the gray
water filling the porthole on the right—
a long gray pause. Then letting in the white.
"The princess wonders why the boat seems so
much heavier today." And then the left
takes its own gray turn. "The soldier danced
with each of them unseen. . . . 'Who danced with me?' "
The ocean is just doing standard ocean;
and the ginger-ale so imperturbably bubbles
filigree weightless trails as in a scene
in a paperweight where the obliging ship
pulls away, over and over again
while the tiny good-byes float up. Good-bye!
Somehow, the story's pleasure loses me,

somehow. "When one had a cup of wine in her hand,
he drank it up." Jon and I split it after,
but it had gone flat. That night, the ship escaped
through a trapdoor in the bedroom floor
to pirouette from prince to prince to prince
till partnering all twelve of them at once,
and I, who could never be happy at a dance,
I slept sound, worn out from all that rocking.

Vanity

You tell someone, on your uncomfortable bus,
"You are beautiful." Not someone you have
anything to gain from—you are a girl,
or would be called a girl, and the beautiful
woman in her late sixties, or maybe early
seventies sits across from you. So you just
tell her. Not, particularly, to make her happy;
not so that she will think well of you.
Certainly not the way someone will have
told you the same thing yesterday, made you feel
alternately—simultaneously—angry and guilty,
guilty because complicit because flattered,
therefore unfairly angry. You use the same
words, without thinking, without noticing.
Do other people notice? Did other people
notice him? Just because they don't move
their heads doesn't mean they aren't paying
attention. Behind her, it is getting dark
enough so you can see yourself out there
through the window. Does it erase what he said,
clear it out, or fill it? You don't want
to be beautiful, you want other people
to be beautiful, and you want to sit
across from them on the bus. Such beautiful
hair, softened and softened, like a fine hankie
washed and washed. My grandmother showed me
on shipboard, in her cabin, a good way to dry
a handkerchief so you don't have to iron it:

you smooth it, wet, against the shower wall;
it leaves the edges a little bit curled over,
like cording on the border of cotton pyjamas.
I saw my grandmother materializing
through the wall in the basement in the new
house, after we came back. She had died
while we were overseas, but she let me know
I didn't have to worry, I could go back
to bed now. From somewhere at the back of the bus,
shrieks, agonized gleeful shrieks, "My KNEES!
God! He'll take one look at my KNEES and puke!"
So that, without even moving our heads
we were reassured, positive he wouldn't.

Gaze

Glued to the set. Winning, the glittery star
of the daytime soap weeps into the mike—she's *there*,

it's a real moment in her real life, and we know it
in spite of the ways she's worked to learn to show it

weeping and glistening, breathy gasps and cries,
stark hospital set, and starry hospital eyes

unbandaged, to the cure of long-lost love,
and her speech of heartfelt thanks—*our* moment of

Say it, what *we* would say, our unmouthed hopes—
but we sound just like a character from the soaps,

she does and we do, speeches like SweeTarts
cheap jazz on the tongue, chalk in the teeth, our hearts

popping unredeemed and soapy against the gloss
we reinstate to wall us from our loss.

Answers

America is about as POPULAR CULTURE
as you can get so far
as I know.
There is no question about POPULAR CULTURE.

POPULAR CULTURE is nonstop 24 hours a day
 continuous
rock video—MTV. We play it for company
when no one is home.
Easy

to be delighted
or dismayed by POPULAR CULTURE
but then one has no other option and even
"God, it's so dreadful we watch it because it can't help

being funny" is
to be delighted. It is
what they all say anyway.
POPULAR CULTURE is

assumptions about our senses
of humor
and nostalgia.
Of course Bruce Springsteen is POPULAR CULTURE

with his cars.
Of course he is not.

Laser discs are not POPULAR CULTURE; they are
   technology.
It is not a fine line.

When you want POPULAR CULTURE you don't always
recognize it.
It isn't you, but you keep it
up.

I wanted a hula hoop.
I was not Saturn ringed with continuous shoop-the-shoop,
I was America with my hula hoop.
There is no question about America.

Up Fish Ranch Road

Insects in the pith munching there or out there
zeroing in, zeroing in again—
bunches of birds are arguing cheez-whiz,
geez, gee-whiz, they insist on nonsense,
but the insistence persists, under-
standably, as the cars sing by, deep in
their throats
not to please themselves but because they have to to
keep going. Requisite propulsion.
Even the shifting eucalyptus trunks
give a lean
creak
Hey kiddo miss sheerly rude sit on it
while the squirrels in these tiny branches
overload and scramble. The unmanageable commotion
resists collaboration: which means up
at the zenith oho this rough saw's
my breath

Lining

Where was she? Tucked high
up under the tin roof,
the room half eave-closet
under the raining tin pellets,
the fine tines of rain. Not asleep.
Tiny pins continuing

past no particular view—
more particular. This is the mind's
right, this division. Even to
feed the full air
through the little eye-
javelin and grip-teeth

meticulously splitting
division into itself, its one
dimension, the line
we can't draw. It's not
that she is losing, but
there is no holding

her, nothing for her
to hold. If she could lift
the window these wires
would thread right through
and show no puncture.
There is a question

of pain. Or permeability
to question. Sometimes
the mind rains through,
its percussive this-es,
all its silver skewers
pins in a map

minutely displacing the map;
so not this, paper
obscure through the glitter.
She isn't here, but around
here, in a deep rain
disappearing.

The Lower Cottage

Dug into the hill, so that
sometimes dirt comes down
between the back wall
and the low roof,
and hill-water seeps through
the stone—front light

having to brush through
all the branches,
and a tree-root terrarium
in the bathroom window,
roots thick as your wrist.
Our bed just fits;

when I tuck in the covers,
I skin my knuckles,
and I have to lumber
over you to get out.
Rain on this roof
is softened,

but the squirrels thud
and tumble, cats rebound,
every sound thickens;
and in the middle of the night
haunch against the window,
club rumble in the yard,

        the raccoons loom
         into their shadows
    or anything like a big animal
           on the roof,
         softer, but heavier,
            closing in.

CRACKS

The broken lock, the eaves—
anything can get in—

but what would they want here
but to get out again—

trapped and flapping in fear
or anger or hunger or pain

toward some dumb warmth and this
busily useless brain?

Anything can get in—
the wind, a bad idea—

a *good* idea—but what
is there to feed it here?

Over the cores and seeds
the squirrels crouch and chuff—

they crack the feeder pane—
they chew the wood like grass—

Enough! You've had enough!
One nuthatch kibitzes—

(nuthatch—what a name!)
the titmouse knocks and knocks—

again it knocks and knocks—
one seed against the frame.

TRACKS

The tracks stop, and I wake up. *I jumped, it seemed?*
"Get off the lawn," and so I jumped and woke up?

No, he said, "*Not on* the lawn." The blades, of course,
had been slicing through the snow, which can't have been

very thick because greeny grass tufted through it and
it was gravelly, dimpled, pocked. So I wasn't *skating*

on thin ice but on thin snow. The problem with thin
ice is that when the tracks stop you cave in,

but with thin snow the damage is to the ground.

The wish in the dream is that if I didn't think

of damaging the ground it wouldn't be hurt

and that as soon as I was warned of it
I and all possible damage would disappear—

easily, not as I'd have to in *real life*,
stumbling and gouging to harder ground—but to rise

out of the genre altogether. I know I hadn't
done damage because I can *see* the tracks, clean, just in

the surface, not what they'd have to be: cuts *through* snow,
grass, mud, now smeared and bleeding into each other.

Conscience Rocks

i. Petrified Forest

Silt, mud, and volcanic ash. Silica deposits.
Part of me thought there would really be a forest.

Green. And I know which forest, too, because it's
Vertigo, Kim Novak in disguise

wandering through the redwoods stops to rest
at the framed cross-section: through her eyes

see history in concentric rings—Columbus
disembarks, three fingers away we sign

the Declaration . . . Slowly, "Here I was born,"
she carries us on her fingertip and sighs:

"and here I died." *Columnar light and nimbus
underwater, deep and luminous stone.*

ii. The Catch

In my revisionist *Vertigo*, he never
discovers the incriminating necklace.

There is no moment when he works the clasp
and it clicks, glittering in his eyes: he *knows*.

And so no second and resolving drive
down the grim coast and up the dizzy tower

releases her or breaks her; but instead
she stiffens—beautiful contortionist—

in hopeful guilt, in charitable deceit
attempting reperfection. *Still yourself*

into the woman that he thought she was
so you can kill the woman that you were—

in slow, perpetual torment as he keeps
on recreating her out of your reach.

iii. Desert Night

Lay not up for yourselves treasures upon earth,
where moth and rust doth corrupt,
and where thieves break in and steal:

But lay up for yourselves treasures in heaven,
where neither moth nor rust doth corrupt,
and where thieves do not break through nor steal:

for where your treasure is,
there will your heart be also.

The light of the body is the eye:
if therefore thine eye be single,
thy whole body shall be full of light.

But if thine eye be evil,
thy whole body shall be full of darkness.
If therefore the light that is in thee be darkness,
how great is that darkness.

iv. In This Case

Not loot. Not amethyst
in crystal fist-chunks, quartz
torn from the trunk-guts—just
indifferent, splintery bits

of rock like weathered rust
or rain-corroded leather,
dull chips (they'd be lost
on a desk-top). Here together:

the little things we wanted
it couldn't hurt to take,
could it? We took for granted
our ease in taking. *Make*

us whole! the little letters
almost weep. "We want
to send these back —our father
had them—well, we found

them when we had to clear
the house out, when he died."
Or: "I couldn't tell my husband,
and I lied

when they asked us at the gate
as we left the park—"
the park itself too late
established in the dark

aftermath of plunder: come and see
where the petrified forest
used to be.
Impurity

in the wood will petrify
and harden,
only to be hacked out.
Surely we wish it were in our power to pardon—

we who read
the notes in the "Conscience Display"
don't read snidely, greedily—we need,
we *want* to know what to say—

I do. Nobody mocks
the un-ironic wife,
her "marriage on the rocks,"
this "moment in her life"

—a moment like crystal,
crystal broken into broken lights—
the moment she fastens on "to set
to rights."

FRANCESCA & PAOLO

          "the punishment is in the skin"

"Self-pity is the punishment in the sin
of vanity. And in the sin of wanting
always to be right, the punishment
is knowing it isn't possible.
                             Is it?
I can't help it. This is what I want

now, Paolo, Paolo, for Paolo to remember
suddenly one thing that he made and wants
to hold to.
             Now, while the foam-flecked horses rear
to harsh cartoony piping—let him torque
towards the brass ring, and *rear*—
                                   No!
                                    he's a bird!
We're birds, he's a bird, he's a bird;
                                we knit the air,
we knit the air between us with that book:
pages, wind-whipped,
                       and the spine at an angle
that proves it will always open
to the same place, bent by need
for the next thing.
                    'They read no more that day.'

Oh, I don't need you
to hate yourself,

as I hate myself, half still gone—so what?—
to you. My particular circle moves
faster, tighter, on one pinned wing.
Don't pity me,

sin, keep reading, keep something—
                             yes, self-pity
is vanity and wants punishment and wants knowing
it isn't and isn't *paolo, paolo, paolo.*"

Picnic

1.

You can't choose
what you throw away.
Can you?

The weeds in the heap
you let drop
past the garden's edge
burn
a bare patch in the lawn.

Later, you will bury a flicker.
Later, you bury a finch.

2.

Timothy cries and cries
and yet keeps hugging up
his baby fists, full
of banana,
sticky with bees.

Would you look at Jenny on the see-saw?
She must be older: she *flings*
her bitten apple
into the pit.

              Is that sad?
I'm thinking, "sweet, grainy spit,"
like remorse;
              or thinking, of course,
"relief."

But, no, the scary bit gathers
its six-legged prickle, and wings
back to her lips.
Clings.

II

Songs of Multiplication and Division

Thou Art Translated

for Anthony

1

I want my palm to keep falling
over the silk, assuming,
infinitely assuming some equal sheen.

The wall, the pool, set up these expectations.
The high wall, and the lozenge-shaped celadon pool
imply the garden, the vista vast as sheer

logic in which the *stayres, degrees, or goings up* are polished,
invisible, assumed.
I want my hand to keep falling

and then to skim the pool,
the lozenge-shaped celadon pool with the trilled border,
the terraces, the complicated rose

trellises that grow or swing together,
the vines and trompe l'oeil vines of painted wood.
The silk is too fine. The surface infinitesimally prickles

against my skin and in this air
sewn through with spiders, hovering,
shriveled in dead curls, like bits of old leaf. They do not die

against the wall or drop. They snag
in the various blurs and glitters, the old stickiness,
and no web.

2

I am a lozenge, a trill, a vine
painted on wood. *A line
is a right consecutive imagination*

*in length, beginning at a poynt, and endeth also at a point,
but it hath no bredth.* I am talking to you about a picture or
   a
principle. You might say,

"The spiders are our friends." They lived in the cracks
in the dock, so I didn't hang my legs down.
Or I was startled up from the water, the tiny ambush

of octagon flexed pin-points over the surface.
Or these are the spiders you harbor in your house.
It's our house, the spiders are our friends.

*You must work round about
from step to step, always following
this rule, by the which you cannot fail,*

says Serlio, on shadows, "Translated
out of Italian into Dutch and out of Dutch
into Englifh. Entreating of Perfpective

which is, Infpection, or looking into,
by fhortening of the fight." I have shewed
many kinds of goings up,

3

but there are other kinds. I would like to rely
on the grand geometric assurances
one could voice in 1611—a line

a plan, its implementation. Things from another time
or in translation welcome
an understanding of something

that is not there,
that insinuates, proliferates like honeysuckle
painted over wood. The imprisoning trellis

does not correspond.
The spiders do not correspond.
These are not the extravagant dead hedges

of the castles of the Loire during that gray March,
nor our wedding garden. But it is one and the same
right consecutive imagination

denying and reconstructing,
so the honeysuckle quickly coils the Loire,
the wedding, your voice, the lake, and even

denial into the dream.
The interrupted vista swings out,
and the hungry, hungry focus gobbles you up.

4

Let me introduce you to
Vitruvius, Serlio, Robert Peake, Inigo Jones,
if not the absent gardener. They won't say the border

is Doubt or Gravity or Sleep; or here is the rose,
here asphodel. Both architects and workmen are advised,
however, in a "Treatise of Scenes, or places to play in,"

that *You may also make Images, Histories, or Fables
in Marble against the wall, but to represent the life
they ought to stirre.* It is the eye alone

stirring. These orchestrations of my right,
far-sighted eye, this distant, scrupulous detail,
unscrupulous, like Röschen's fairy-tale hedge,

keep us out. I want you to walk in the garden.
It is ours. I have been my whole life privileged,
as everyone, by its effortless, unpredictable construction;

but I only arrive through invitation or dazzling
abduction, or something between them like your
proposal in Prospect Garden. Love, attend.

We cannot carve or forcibly preserve
or cultivate belief. If it will grow, it grows
as we do—mostly after we have fallen

5

asleep. Like swimming through the telescope,
assume the rare and unprecarious focus.
There is no railing at the top of the core,

a tall cylinder with a willow's long green leaves,
rushing slowly, smoother than willow as I fell
through a soft fear, all the foreground breath;

and the green was the color of motion
past green on film, my arms opening
and closing through continuous kimonos

of lighter green. As I grew lighter,
the green took on more body
like seemingly freeform bodies:

wind, waves, scarves swaying
inside my arms. How do I believe the simultaneous
translation, the seamless grafting

as leaves now flow into scarves, now halfway down,
balloon silk, a pale flamingo pink, billowing
counter the fall, delaying the fall;

plume; equilibrium. Here I am.
Here you are. In my repertoire of dreams,
the first happy fall. Unasked,

6

I am completely given and given
back
complicated and unqualified

the cool and incredible silt
accumulating against the man-made walls
of Little Falls Creek. I would slide down

to try to take it from the water. Soft,
and softer than the water, than the air,
it filtered through my fingers and it slid

from underneath my toes. It must taste good.
It must taste like milk. There were willows there.
I come up from the dream. Do you know how,

sometimes, when you first wake up,
your pulse is so thorough, so slow,
that you, and the one who is with you,

and the room, and the opening light all seem to swell
and subside and swell inside your heart?
How you could rise to the window and discover

the lawn, Cedarwood Drive, and the sky independently
   dreaming
or easing awake, breathing in the hold
of some heart newer, larger than your own?

Distant Heart

What is the shape made there
where the lingering red bird sings
from a branch let free to steady
itself, and two last leaves
clinging, reverberate
imperfectly matching red
when he launches into cold air—
what is the shape made there?

FLIGHT

The bat careers
—a quicker shark—
precisely veers
a re-zoned arc

but like a kite
precipitate
the string works taut
to choke acute

the upswept silk
Let go the hand
(if it could talk)
Let go the wind

not to ascend
but to erase
like silk, like sand
the path, the force

dissolving mica
intricate
I land—glint—wait
for me to find.

Adam's Hand

"or Michael taking Adam by the wrist"

Is that when Adam has to leave the garden?
Does Adam's hand hang down? Is Michael cruel,
or does he think if he took Adam's hand
it might seem like a comfort, cruelly seem
like something else for Adam to let go?
And Eve, who isn't mentioned in the poem,
I picture Eve with both hands clasped behind her,
some way behind the angel and her husband,
but not lagging behind. Nobody speaks.
And when they hear the rustling in the grass,
which cannot be Eve's dress, since Eve is naked,
Adam sweats. But Eve? My Eve remembers
the sliver of apple underneath her tongue,
the sticky imprint left in Adam's palm.

Song of Multiplication and Division

> O wonderful! O wonderful! O wonderful!
> I am food! I am food! I am food!
> —Taittiriya Upanishad

Come down the hill,
past the humming renovations,
past the white house holding the promise of dough rising
three times into the night and into the morning,
loaves, soon, for the neighbors,
come down soon,

down the steep crumbling curve of the gravel drive
and come next spring: new peonies rising,
next summer's blackberries surge in the bare brambles,
come under those hummocks groundhogs,
moles, snakes, shrews.
                      So mint will return,
and the sudden asparagus. Soon I
will sit by my window, rocking. Just outside,
the birds fight at the feeder. Seed hulls ping
from time to time against the glass.
                                The albino cardinal
haunts the rhododendron, redoing songs. She sings:
Somewhere inside another seed takes flight.
The rhododendron blooms. Come flower flower.
Seed, seed. The sun says your body is milk, your baby
   swims.

The pine says your baby milks your swimming body.
The mole says swim with your baby in the milky way,
one milky body.

One seed hull splits and pings against the glass.

The snake in his sleep says, so, the room is ready.
Divide, divide.
                        But I sit by the window
rocking my baby. He can see chickadee
sweep patio to feeder, flip from cord
to perch, go greedily after seed.
                                        He sees
these shapes as separate from the winter blur.
Alert.
           The dun deer that will cross the yard
to nibble the dutch iris calls to my baby.
The raccoon, who, upside down from the rail contrives
to grab from its hook and disengage the feeder,
to smash it like a cookie jar for seeds, calls to my baby.
Even the cat, who sleuths through the snow
to bring me the shrew with blood on her head,
calls to my baby. O, come eat! come be!

Private, Offhand Sestina

In the beginning, there was long division
of the literate body from the musical soul;
in the beginning there was this and that;
in the long beginning there were too
many things to count on the fingers of one hand
so there were two hands, oh translucent fingers,

proof of nectar, traced by light, and fingers
tracing boundaries of no more division,
but coming together. This scar on the back of my hand:
a compass puncture. What circles the soul
now anchors, love. This is a circle, too,
one more ring around the olive tree that

Ulysses built his bed from, the bed that
Penelope chose as his test, how many fingers
am I holding up? Of course, she made that bed, too,
and lay down in it, lay down in division
from herself, unraveling the sail
she wove for cover and might have kept, one hand

steady on the loom, but the other unsteady hand
like a flag part-freed by the wind, rip-fluttering; that
hand works to undo the work done by her soul.
Then both hands in her lap, still. Useless fingers.
I am not wife, not widow, live division
of loss from expectation of loss. Then, too,

I have my son; I have my son. Then, too,
the weave might someday hold, work of this hand
take sheen, complete, of infinite division
become dimension. Like the spider's silk that
looses its balloons. (Two calloused fingers
hold his pen. I miss you, oh my soul.)

What am I talking about? Never my "soul,"
but you gave me my body, and I miss that too.
Sam points O's on the globe with baby fingers,
O for Ocean. Atlantic, Pacific. His hand
spanks and spins the pale blue world with a THAT
and a THAT, new O O O. And then, division—

"High reach Moon!" (hands high)—what is division?
"High reach Clouds!" I hold him high as my soul
dares risk. He counts: "O, Clouds! O, one and my two!"

The Anguish

Anguish is vacuum, or the vampire—returning
to the whispering puncture where you hide,
hunched into your body—who can come

as a shadow wolf behind you and the wolf
who pads on, shadowless, or as the bat who veers
and flaps against your face, or as the mist

feeding through your closed window on the air,
an irresistible lung without its lung,

looking for forms, a real body to inhabit.
How greedy it is to suck forms into itself,
any set shape, any incontestable hardness.

This belongs to me and this is mine;
and if this was here before, this was to prove
that I would come. This will not be itself
without me after.
                    Oh, hungry for absolutes,
this impossible cross, the abstract ore become
a silver bullet, what is my seeking to that

insatiability? Bit by bit we come
to gather the homely about us, a wreath of good
garlic, a bone sufficient for soup, the copied

recipe we can't get quite right but keep
on trying. So, I'm not enough. I'm saved.

LEAVE-TAKING

Which of us will cry first, me or the house?
Soberly, placidly, off and on, glistening
over the old trails. How it holds over us

(here where marriage seems like a promise to keep
overflowing a small space) drifts on drifts
of web. Its spiders ravel the rafter shadows,

draw the walls down, intending—what? It only
knows, heavily, to hold us while we sleep.
While we sleep, the door warps in its frame.
Moss veins the front stoop, fretting the old stone.

(The different mosses.) Grass catches back from its falling
plumes, and holds in their parting, dew. You be

a statue. I'll be the little finished fountain
catching only the leaves, and rain.

Thread of Song

How would you take a stitch in time?
And where is the boy who looks after the sheep?

The blackberry bleeds on your thumb, bleeds voice.
Come blow your horn. Where is the thorn?

Come save the nine lives kittens lost
the mother's voice, the cloud, the rain,

the rain in needles. Needles lost
under the haystack, fast asleep.

A stitch to keep. Keep time. Keep time.

Mock Sestina

Hush little baby don't say a word
Mama's gonna buy you a mocking bird
Remind her of songs someone picks up
Like pretty pebbles in a cup
Amethyst quartz or mundane clay
Lose the cup or throw it away

If that mocking bird—*away*—
don't sing a solitary word
Mama's gonna make one out of clay
enthralling bird performing bird
perched on the brim of a silver cup
beat with a silver spoon look up

at the singing bird sweetheart look up
before it flies—*don't sing*—away
Mama melt down that silver cup
and forge little baby a diamond word
a diamond ring You want the bird
The ring turn brass You want the clay

Mama want hush little dust into clay
Mama's gonna buy you make it up
Looking glass fly back the bird
Looking glass give you away
You looking for the turning word
Fly back handle to the cup

Get broke keep the broken cup
Hush little mud much better than clay
Mud don't break don't break you word
You billy goat will pull you up
Won't pull won't pull just go away
Mama's gonna buy you a mocking bird

A cart and bull a cart and bird
Fly you a wish a bird and cup
Drink you angry thirst away
Fall over dog and throat like clay
Hoarse little stunned glass bird fly up
Sing backover breakneck note no word

No don't don't Mama won't bark brick cup-
board shut up wind blows rock and clay
Treetop   rockward   mockaway

ECHOLOCATION: THE WHALE

In Jonah's nightmare, everybody cries
or rages,
or cries out against some rage,
or sins unthinking. "O, what meanest thou?"
cry the sailors when they find him in the hold,
asleep. "What meanest thou? arise and call
upon thy god."
                  I saw you in the womb—
that much seems certain—or I saw a ghost-
baby sucking its ghost-thumb in the gray
newsreel from some future moon so far
the light wears out in breathing itself back
to us. It's hard to read. The forms emerge
flickering in cross-sections of motion.
The only thing we're sure of is the heart,
its constant pulse. And then the empty space
of the skull.
            If reason wants to take us in
to Jonah's rage, some way into the slow
accumulating cry he cried "by reason"
of his own sore affliction, into waters
that compassed him about even to the soul,
into the depth that closed him round about,
and thick into the lash and clutch of weeds—
then where do we find ourselves but sinking, sinking?
Reason, water, depth and weeds.
                        My soul
fainted within me

                    When I hear the shrieks
of the child—my child?—and then the deeper voice,
a father's voice in anger—is it his?—
zeroing in on me from down the street,
it's glorious to realize they're not mine,
a greedy relief. At least it is at first,
but they keep on, and then I have to see,
and crack the blind. The father leads, head down,
as if to batter a wall. "Shut up! shut up!"
Each time he just can't hold it he lets loose.
"Shut up!" The child, about a leash-length back,
a jerked leash, howls obliteration, howls
and dawdles, miserably. I know this dance,
mundane, bitter and intimate. "Shut up!"
As if some weed or tentacle has yanked
him round, the father lunges at the child
and yells—but it's too funny—what he yells
this time is "Donuts!" hauling the hoarded sweet
deep from the clutched sack. "Donuts!" But the child
still blots the world with howls. "God dammit! Take them!
Shut up! You're driving me fucking nuts!"
                                        I've let
the blind fall long since.
                          Jonah dreams a god
who wants to hold him and sing lullabies.
As if sweet reason comforted enough,
as if our feeble reasons comfort you,
as if our knowing you should comfort us.
So Jonah's god then spake unto the fish.
It vomits Jonah out upon dry land.

LESSON

I thought once I knew he was "gone," that I
could see him here and not still feel the dis-

engaging. As a guest removes his coat

on entering, and leaves his life outside,
narrowing like the light in the doorway, down

from two dimensions to one, then to no point

that I could see. I'd only have to admit
so much of him. Indent, but not inhabit.

He wouldn't inhabit my life, it wouldn't cling

to him, dragging at his sleeves and ankles,
snagging his heel. A shadow in a well-

loved children's book despairs: the soap he wants

to stick him to his body slips away.
Might as well ask a house to choose which light

not to admit, there, pouring in the door.

MINE

1.

I think you might need to know this about me.
I'm still standing
in the doorway of the master bedroom
in a house that I might live in
and the man with the gun
says it's hot
and shoots
again.

2.

I didn't know about the horseback ride,
breakneck, urged by a crazed guide, right to the brink
of the crater. The two of them,
right at the crater's brink.

3.

He shoots the door. "Hot," he says again.
And later, he recapitulates. We travel
back through the unsafe house.
This door is hot
and this and this.
This windowsill's okay.

And this new wall's completely safe, but here
where they've kept the old door, none of this new paint
will make a difference; this door's off the charts.

4.

I think you should know this about me, that for me
all doors are hot.
If you call that sensitive
instrument you use to register levels
of lead in the walls "a gun," I'll think of guns.
If you press your palm, gently, against the cherished
antique door and utter, flatly, "hot,"
then I'll think *hot*. I can't not see your hand
begin to glow,
to shrink back for you from
invisible seething.
A palm against the forehead of a child;
the voice, the doctor's, says a kid can take
a heat we can't. Veering, the hummingbird
siphons the bright red feeder's sugar water.
The speedy heart. Hot house. A fine airborne
particulate, and the tender fiddlehead fern,
the baby orchid of the two-year-old brain,
all vessels and filaments, susceptible
to that sick sifting. Reasons. A sixth sense—
the sense of metaphor. So now you only
really see you're safe
where some latecomer finally chose to strip
right down to the grain.
A different finish.
Hope for stain.

5.

Somewhere about him the man must keep
a tea strainer for the kidney stone.

Keep away from what went into this.
And then, much later, suffer from the crumbling
deficiencies. And from the invisible
mold, from dust motes in the pillows. From
a tiny, mimosa-like blossom, the elephant
hears a Who. The paper wrapper whispers
from the scalpel. Without anesthesia, he
lances the vaginal abscess. Light, like a paper
airplane flies to the back of her throat. I think

6.

you might need to know this about me. When I fell
I blacked out, and the shutter clicked. I lost
an eye. I think that you might need to know
this about me. I cut myself and tell
no one, but draw the picture: pencil dust
shines silver from the page. I think you might
need to know this about me. I direct
the runway planes,
I know where they should go,
and when the helicopters flatten the house
with shattering beams,
you need to hide under the stairs.
I think you might need to know this about me—my heart—
I can hear it inside me,
but I can't see it.
I know
I'll see it when it comes out.

7.

You need to know that for me, all doors are hot.
I'll put my hand right through the pane and miss
the material for the metaphor, the tangible

for the tangent. I'm not listening to you,
I'm listening to what you say.
I think you need to know
that when he goes
through the house laying hands on things
and saying "hot, now nothing, now hot—"
it's like some kind
of mine he's checking for, a water witch
reversing wells we might have wanted—this
is no place for a spring.
My heart's too big
for his chest. They race.
My water breaks. The sweet
red feeder. Don't talk, mommy, he says to me.

8.

He wants me in the crib. A cat in a cage
excretes considerable quantities
of sugar in its urine when it hears
a dog barking nearby. "Emotional
glycosuria." I'll disappear.

9.

I think you might need to know this about me. I can't
hear straight and every door is hot. My doors
are hot and shut.
I can't find the door in heat
mirages. My heart's too big for his chest.
We crash and race against each other until
he says, mommy, just sleep.
But you, when I want you most
I don't want you. Release
of epinephrine in the bloodstream. Sweetly,

it crawls, the flesh, the dark. We are still standing
in the doorway of a master bedroom.
My grandparents honeymooned on Vesuvius.
A pickle jar exploding through the glass.
Don't touch the paint in blisters. There is some-
thing. Sizzle of sperm. The flat of the back.
I would have kept on going down the road,

whatever road, it was hot, but the men in the truck,
and the heat pools under the trees. Behind my back,
when the plane tilts, fire and down until—
no will, no one to care for the child—
letters, letters,
looping illegibly, underwater
flowers released from tiny capsules, dye
drifting up, the brand name on the film
scrolling before home
movies, letters on the runway—you
won't kill yourself. When he wasn't dying yet,
it was Italian,
over and over, Italian, I want to die.

10.

Again, at the brink,
off the charts, some hope for stain.
I'll never have another bed. I think
when it comes out, don't talk, I'll disappear.
All words are doors, all doors are hot, all heat
is flesh, all flesh is grass, so look for me
under your bootsoles, under your bloody boots.
I can hear you—why can't you hear me?
I'm nobody you know and I'm still standing.

Ohio: Unused Fireplace

Little, leather-ships in ocean-deep
rooms, the bats swoop
down the study chimney,
dining room chimney, bedroom, living room,
that first, most unmoored year,
renting the "Bishop's Palace."

The next year, in our new house,
how can I choose
to christen the glassed-in fireplace
while he sweats in apartment overheat
or rides a Berkeley mountain-bike on ice
through Minneapolis?

Third year of exile, I go bats,
ride the exercise bike, steal fuel
from overheated brain, furnish
the womb, demand a clown
quilt to flap down over the fireplace,
upstairs, for the baby's room.

Fourth year, all here, and not
at all all here—what fool
brandishes fire beside her milky boy,
beside herself; the firescreen glares
or gleams, screeches and swallows
dust.

Year five, not here, we split
and disappear. The baby sings
"Fire fire, says Obediah,"
draws helping strings.
What's fear?
What's fair?

Year six, back, fix
what can be fixed,
ignore the front-yard trench, for now,
wrench yourself—
you can make the heat
stick to the wall with paint,
don't say you can't.

A Company

Seems like a different window. In the morning:
"teakettle" wren and cardinal,
finches, finches, chickadee-dee, a bustle
bearing the light to the feeder,
arrowing back to the sky:

light as a crowd of birds, a company.

At night, the "prowler" light
makes a solo world
appear
out there
on the other side of the dim glare,
sketch-light of my writing
at the table.

Spotlight: then the hobo skunk,
hobo opossum, garbage-cleaner tramps
sort through seed-hulls underneath the feeders—
all odd lumbering nonchalance
and twitchy discrimination—

though, no, the skunk is neater
on its feet, and, efficiently fierce,
nips a three-inch jag in a garbage bag
to extract Hunan mu-shu. (He's so small,

often he doesn't trip the light at all.)
And the possum moves so low.

The only inhabitants of some "dark out there,"
staged as allegory. Too small to be
dangerous. Too big for a rat—that naked, thumb-thick tail.

Lonely, hungry, fierce, pathetic, obsessed
(five of my seven dwarves), and then the pained
progress of one I haven't seen before,
or not like this.
It moves wrong. It's not right,

not right as if the radar's skew,
as if it thinks sick; it half-heaves
into view, effort of
stiff joints, limbo-bones
able to turn
on you but not stand up
for itself, beseeching but looking
away or looking blind,
one mid-size raccoon. Rabid,
one has to think, it's on the list;
a world-size thirst and throat too small,
it keens to drink
air through the ear—
is thrown

from that thirst only to ask
*is it you? is it you
who throws this thirst on me?
it will bite you too, such teeth—
I won't let go,*

*I'll bite the sky you breathe,
I bit the moon,
I'll bite you soon.
I'll bite you soon.*

But, no, mere bodily hunger drives this beast,
and the psycho-gait's explained—

the back right leg's
a stump, and so's the tail.
This is the numb
stumbling of a creature who has to come
hungering through the impossibility
of grace, or maybe I'd have to say its usual grace,

since what looks awkward is in fact the best
animal efficiency—it serves;
and what look like mistakes,
corrective swerves. Illness of body overhauled
by a mind less than some
inclined to question its clear
and present task, removing itself
from place to place to place.
It sweeps the seeds

then turns to the window and looks me in the face.

Birdnotes

In the village, a single bird can be an event,
can be news—just as the appearance
of an available heterosexual male
between the ages of 22 and 60
can be news. It is news here, for example,
when a Baltimore oriole shows up at the feeder,
or a scarlet tanager (a pair of them!).
It is news that the pileated woodpecker
sits on the car in the driveway at seven each morning
pecking and pecking away at his imagined
competitor in the sideview mirror—news,
at any rate, that the mirror hasn't broken
like those on all the other cars in range;
to challenge the neighbors' brand-new silver Volvo,
the woodpecker flew *into* their garage.
So their mirrors now sport plastic bags,
rubberbanded to them as in some
science experiment protecting flowering
trees from pollination. Even so,
not all birds are events. They come, they go.
But then that poor lost emu on a rampage
through the village—definitely news,
more so when finally lassoed by the chair
of the Philosophy Department. We
all have news to write to sweethearts, far
away from here, living in cities. See,
we can write with gravity, "Birds are news."
But these are some of the things that constitute

village life. Now, it is summer, and while
I sit by a river (I'm away;
it's not the village river, named for the owls,
but the kind of river that constitutes
city life, along which, summer Sundays,
they block the street to traffic)—
                              Did I tell you
that *other* piece of bird news, when Linda and I
drove out of the village on a Saturday night
for dinner at a small-town restaurant—
roast pork & mashed potatoes, chicken & noodles,
your choice of sides: beans, coleslaw, tapioca—
while we were eating, in come Jane and Perry
and Peggy and Tom, and they want to know
if we have seen the herons. No? They tell us
where to find them, lend us their binoculars.
So, twilight, from the side of the road, I count
two dozen nests, I think, in two great trees:
all eerie charcoal Rorschach: birds emerge
against the sketchy branches as they shift
their stilts. Much squawking. Linda says she sees
the babies lifting their beaks. It's news, it's news.
Now, here, with the riverside traffic blocked so folks
on bicycles and rollerblades glide by—
a brightly-colored, mushroom-helmeted species,
many with the characteristic black
fingerless gloves and shiny kneepads, gliding
by in packs, in ones, twos—this one, now,
skates past my bench in purple sleeveless T,
sky-blue shorts, white baseball cap. She carries
a cup of coffee from Au Bon Pain. There, perched
easily on the brim, her orange parrot
looks on the world with a somewhat jaded eye,
for this is a city—and this is not news,
this is nothing, isn't it? Nothing I
or anyone would write home from the city
to my sweetheart, in the village, if I had one.

Landscape Lit by an Apricot

This is how it's supposed to arrive,
                        like this—
after a long dark spring, late in rainy summer,
the afternoon skies about to gather themselves
to go down to the river—
                  here,
                          at the corner
of Putnam and Green, the otherwise unseen tree
reveals itself as an apricot—
                        the fruit
is ripe—
    ripe, multiple and overflowing
the box set just outside the fence. The sign
says, "take!"
You can hardly take it—
how you want
to wait there, leaning slightly over the fence,
to watch for the next to ripen and let go
into your palm. Such pleasure, looking up
into nothing but green—
                      then one, a moon—
then four, like a cluster of pale yellow eggs in a nest—
apparition like proof, or like belief.
You want to be here.
                    This summer, mother and child
take in, in the enormous dark, their first
movie together, *James and the Giant Peach*.

Right from the start, he's on her lap, she holds
him tight, he can't let go—
                              he's terrified
and *wants* to be,
                there where light arrives
and arrives in particles,
                              arrives in waves
on a beach and travels up a rocky shore
to the desolate attic from which the hungry child
looks out on a spindly tree:
                              it will balloon
with the magic fruit
                    into whose heart
                                    he'll climb
and feed,
          and then in which they will take flight
over the ocean, as if to fulfill the wish
of the lost father.
                    And yet, to be held to earth
by hunger, sharing hunger, now. No fruit
shows brown on the tree, and none lies bruised,
none rots on the velvet lawn. The invisible tender
sees to it all,
              sees that the bright globes keep
on filling up with light,
                        even while we sleep.

Ruth's Garden

The Spanish brought the trumpet-shaped petunia
and lemons from the Andes. Nineteen-ten
saw eucalyptus and wisteria.
Montbretia shoots up lush at winter's zenith.
Under the fuschia bells, hummingbirds hover
and dangle like fishing lures. My neighbor offers
over her side-yard fence, an enormous bunch
of spinach, trailing its sturdy, dirt-crumbed root.
"*Take* these; I just let them all go old."
And then, when I thank her, "It's really no big deal."
But I have to think I haven't heard her right
when she lets drop "in vitro fertilization—"
Surely she's talking technology for her garden,
for the tiny, pear-baby yellow and red tomatoes,
the plum and beefsteak jostling to bursting
the paper sack that she left on my doorstep.
This year she's trained the tomatoes over a frame.
But no, she says, she's been looking at pictures of triplets,
which happen sometimes, looking at pictures of twins.
Casually, as she restakes the little front fence
protecting her wildflowers, she says only one
in four works out at all. It's always seemed to me
she could grow anything. In the fairy tale
the wife's craving sends her husband over the wall
to plunder the witch's garden. And in the myth,
the young girl secretly cradles in her cheek
five forbidden pomegranate seeds.
And in the pregnant dream, her water breaks

on a pool table, so she starts to drive
herself to the hospital, veers into a field
and—feet on either side of the steering wheel—
gives birth to a boy as constellations glide
and whirl over the dashboard, silver and black
and red, a kaleidoscopic zodiac.
Crouching in her garden, her fingers rake
and soften the dirt. Thistle and meadowfoam,
lupine, thornmint, butterweed, and lily
are all endangered, as are checkerbloom
and live-forever, I think as I discover
dark sugary trails where I've clutched the root to my shirt.

HOUSEHOLD PRAYER

for the Very Reverend W.S.P. & J.G.P.

When I cleaned house for Joy
across from the Golden Gate—
when I cleaned house for Will
on "holy hill"—

it was the house I wanted,
the only house for me—
and Will was religion,
and Joy was poetry:

top-heavy roses,
olive-tree arcade,
and the light was gold-dust clear
like a new Vermeer.

I mopped the kitchen floor,
dusted the glass-topped box
and rows on rows of books,
removed each chair

from the pale, pale blue
carpet so the path
the vacuum made was smooth
as meditation—life

in that household was grace:
what could there be for me
to clean in such a place?
Then, a window pane

relinquished a gray film
to the dust-cloth,
and glass in every room
let go such gray—

I felt the smudge was me
but came to see
that Joy left smoke
on the bedroom vanity.

(And why shouldn't Joy smoke,
for heaven's sake.)

I couldn't tell
what was left after Will
had done his work.
I wonder, still.

Then, on the day the bomb
went off on the other coast
in empty rooms,
I stopped and wrote the first

draft of a poem there,
in poetry's house,
but not in Joy's chair
upstairs with the slow, continuing, sea view,

but at the sermon typewriter,
downstairs,
in choppy strokes—
a poem I still redo,

a poem for my father against time—
as if an act of will,
performed there, in that house,
like clearing glass,

like lifting dust,
a simple, repeating gesture like a rhyme
(without having to try
to save the past)

could marry joy, could really hold and last.